A NATIONAL TRUST BOOK

RARE BREEDS

by
CHRISTOPHER HANSON-SMITH

INTRODUCTION

The public awareness of the threat to the survival of wild animals is now well recognised. The tiger, for example, from being hunted nearly to extinction in the early twentieth century, is now breeding healthily in sanctuaries paid for by Europeans who will never see those fine beasts alive – except in the local zoo.

More belatedly have the same people become aware of the equal urgency for preserving what remains of the stock of rare breeds of domestic animals which, unlike the tiger, are able to be seen on home ground.

In the British Isles since 1972 two breeds – the Irish Dun cow and the Lincolnshire Curly Coat pig – have become extinct. At the start of 1986 there were thirty-nine endangered breeds of livestock, excluding poultry. It is difficult to define a 'breed', which is a race or variety in nature, as a breed is in reality a race manipulated by man to serve best the uses he may have for that particular animal.

As man developed so his needs altered, and the fashions changed. The qualities selected by the breeding process in one century were often not welcome in the next, and the unfortunate or 'uneconomic' cow or sheep was left literally to die out!

Fickle tastes as displayed by the ultimate consumer dictate to the farmer of livestock what type of animals to breed and as fast as tastes alter so do the chances of survival for certain breeds. Like domestic hardware or motor cars, dated models are thrown away with a blind disregard for their true value. The best designs, however, have a habit of resurfacing many years later as 'bygones' or 'antiques' and their value is belatedly appreciated by discerning collectors. How much more important, therefore, to preserve the live 'bygones' within whose bloodstreams are the genes that have developed through centuries of adaptation and the struggle for survival. This genetic bank is unique: once a breed is lost the ability to use those particular genes is also lost. The so-called 'primitive' breeds of sheep have innate qualities which the farmers in many countries may soon come to value highly – the resistance to certain diseases, the ability to produce various naturally coloured wools, and the growth of fleeces which are a match for the worst weather encountered on hill, moor, or marsh.

Sheep-farmers have successfully 'bred out' the hair once found in the fleeces of commercial breeds to produce a wool better suited for spinning and dyeing. The same farmers are now dressing their vulnerable sheep in jackets made from synthetic fibres to keep them warm during harsh winters on the northern fells. Nature had originally provided the ancestors of these same sheep with their own 'jackets' – on the Cumbrian fells the Herdwick breed survives, well insulated against the wet and cold by its own fleece, since it has remained a relatively pure breed, still in possession of a two-layer coat of fine and coarse wool.

The endangered breeds are a living part of our heritage. Visitors are able to witness at an ever-increasing number of farms the Longhorn cattle, for example, that could well have been the breed of dual-purpose cattle used on those same farms two centuries ago. The agricultural museums are full of the utensils necessary to make the butter and till the soil. How much more telling to see the type of cow that produced the milk for the churn, the draught horse that drew the plough, and not forgetting the barnyard fowl that once scratched away at every midden.

The native ponies in particular are part of Britain's heritage and their ancestry can be traced to Neolithic times. The influences of the basic, hardy stock are visible in every riding pursuit whether it be the International Horse Show or classes of riding for the disabled. Two Grand National winners had Exmoor pony blood in their veins and many of today's outstanding children's show ponies derive from Welsh or Dartmoor stock. Likewise the ponies preferred for trekking, a sport that has developed only in the past thirty years, are of the native breeds such as the Fell in Cumbria and the Highland in Scotland.

Now each native breed has its own society with studbook and show classes; and much of the members' time is taken up by telling the public how to appreciate the qualities of a particular breed so that the invaluable reservoirs of native pony blood will never dry up.

It would be wrong to suppose that rare breeds only survive in the British Isles. Throughout the world there remains an enormous and invaluable reserve of genetic resources in the minority livestock breeds. Some native British breeds now only survive or flourish overseas. The loss of breeds has been greatest in countries with well-developed, intensive livestock industries which use advanced breeding techniques. In Norway thirteen native breeds of cattle have become extinct during the past seventy years entirely due to official cattle-breeding policies.

The preservation of those endangered breeds is an international problem as serious as the conservation of wild animals. Public awareness of what is at stake should make sure that no more breeds of domestic livestock are lost for ever.

What is a 'rare breed'?

The Rare Breeds Survival Trust considers four parameters: genetic basis; current trends; feral populations and numbers – to be rare there must be less than the following number of breeding females in the breed: Horses – 1,000, Goats – 500, Pigs – 150, Sheep – 1,500, Cattle – 750. Breeds with four or less distinct male lines will be included in the priority lists. A watching brief is kept by the Trust on breeds with six or less distinct male lines. (A distinct male line is one which has no common ancestors in the last four generations.) Further detail on the priority categories in which each breed is placed can be obtained from the Rare Breeds Survival Trust.

Rare breeds

The list of rare breeds within the British Isles is as follows (January 1986):

HORSES and PONIES

Cleveland Bay
Clydesdale
Exmoor Pony
Suffolk

SHEEP

Boreray
Castlemilk Moorit
Cotswold
Hebridean
Leicester Longwool
Lincoln Longwool
Manx Loghtan
North Ronaldsay
Oxford Down
Portland
Ryeland
Shetland
Shropshire
Soay
Wensleydale
White faced Woodland
Wiltshire Horn

GOATS
Bagot   Golden Guernsey

CATTLE
British White   Kerry
Chillingham   Longhorn
Dexter   Shetland
Gloucester   White Park
Irish Moiled

PIGS
Berkshire   Large Black
British Lop   Middle White
British Saddleback   Tamworth
Gloucester Old Spot

Dales Ponies, Belted Galloway and Red Poll cattle were removed from the lists in 1985.

A note on 'kemp' and 'hair'.

The words 'kemp' and 'hair' appear in the descriptions of several breeds of sheep and it is important, therefore, to define the difference between these two constituents of the fleece.

Kemp is one of two kinds of hairy fibre grown by sheep and derives from the outer coat of the wild ancestor of domestic sheep, that is the Soay, possessed of bristly kemps akin to those of deer, which obscure the short and fine underwool. Kemps are genetic in origin and have a hollow structure which makes them hard to dye.

Hair, in contrast to kemp, is longer, less coarse and much stronger. It is a product of domestication and marks an intermediate stage between kemp and fine wool. Hair responds more both to nutritional and seasonal influences; in summer it is coarse and kemp-like, in winter fine and more like wool.

Both kemps and hair appear most frequently in the fleeces of the hill breeds of sheep and their wool, which is graded as the cheapest unless it can attract a premium for some specialised use such as long-wearing, coarse sweaters. Some kemp is tolerated as it lends distinction to the finest tweeds.

HORSES AND PONIES

Fell Pony This breed has developed on the western slopes of the Pennines and the Dales pony on the eastern side – both breeds were placed in the same category until 1898. They were also known as 'Galloways' from which

Fell Pony

type the Fell may have evolved. Another theory is that the Fell is closely related to the Friesian horse from Holland, either introduced by the Roman garrisons on Hadrian's Wall or Dutch traders at a later date.

Whatever their origin, these ponies became the pack animals indispensable to the trade and industry of what is now Cumbria, North Lancashire, and West Yorkshire. They carried Kendal cloth to Southampton, the journey taking approximately four weeks; coal and iron to the coast; and all manner of goods in their panniers over the fells. The carefully graded pack-horse tracks across the Cumbrian fells and the humped pack-horse bridges are now pleasant routes for the walker to follow. The ponies often travelled in droves of up to twenty, in the charge of one man, and the lead mare wore a collar of bells.

Until 1900 the ponies ran wild on the fells but in 1911 the Board of Agriculture introduced a premium scheme for registered Fell stallions in an effort to improve the breed. These stallions were descended from the fabled Lingcropper, a superb animal whose unknown owner was killed in one of the Border raids in the seventeenth century. This pony ran the mails eighteen miles from Penrith to Keswick for twelve years without a break.

The Fell pony should be constitutionally as hard as iron and show good pony characteristics. The height does not exceed 14 hands and the colour can be black, brown, or grey, with no white markings, although a 'star' is allowed. The mane and tail are not docked and there should be fine hair at the heels.

Today the breed is used as a trekking pony and as an ideal mount for disabled riders. It will be found between the shafts at many driving events all over the country.

Clydesdale Horse

Clydesdale The Shire horse of England and the Clydesdale of Lanarkshire in Scotland both evolved in similar circumstances from an indigenous type of 'Celtic' pony much improved by an admixture of imported blood from Norway, through the Vikings, and from the Continent.

By the early eighteenth century a breed of heavy horse existed in the Lowlands of Scotland and this was further improved by the importation of a black stallion from Flanders. The Clydesdale breed was first mentioned in 1826 and the first stud-book was published by the breed society in 1877.

The Clydesdale is ideally dark brown with a white stripe on the face, dark-coloured forelegs and white hind shanks, but some black horses are seen. The feet are feathered and must be open and round like a mason's mallet. The impression created by a well-built Clydesdale is that of strength and activity, with a minimum of superfluous tissue. It is speedier and less docile than the Shire and requires more handling. The average height of the mare is 16·2 hands whereas the stallions can achieve 17·2 hands.

As a heavy draught horse the Clydesdale is at home both on the farm and in the towns where its freedom from leg troubles is much valued. The breed is well known in many countries, not least in the United States and Canada.

Dales Pony The Dales pony, like the Fell pony, is a native of the Pennines and is sometimes referred to as a 'Pennine' or 'Galloway'. The breeds share a common ancestry and are 'Celtic' ponies.

In 1648 the Allendale lead-mines were established by the Blackett family and at the beginning of this century produced one-quarter of all that mineral mined in England. When horizontal levels were driven into the hillsides they were large enough to admit the Dales

Dales Pony

ponies to tow the tubs containing the ore. From the lead-mines the ponies carried ore, two hundredweight at a time in panniers, to the sailing-ships on the Tyne, thirty to forty miles distant. George Stephenson, who invented the locomotive that eventually took over the work of haulage from the ponies, was himself a pit lad at the Blackett Colliery at Wylam-on-Tyne.

Teesdale was the great pony-breeding area. The animals were bred as sure-footed weight-carriers and fast trotters. They were, therefore, ideal driving ponies and also regarded as excellent family ponies.

The Dales is black in colour but occasionally other colourations, even grey, are found. The height, increased by past crossing with Clydesdales, should not exceed 14·2 hands. The conformation is excellent – a short back with powerful loins, a neat head with small well-placed ears. The feet are very hard and well shaped and the pony's action should be straight and true. There are fine hairs on the heels.

Suffolk The Suffolk breed has remained pure and has a written pedigree only beaten in length by the thoroughbred. But in 1966 the decline in numbers of the heavyweight had been such that only six colts and six fillies were registered. The mechanisation of the flat arable farms in East Anglia was the main cause.

Known also as the Suffolk Punch, a distinct Suffolk type of horse was described by Camden in his *Britannia* in 1506. In 1769 Thomas Crisp, who lived near Woodbridge, in Suffolk, bred a horse from which every present-day Suffolk is descended. Numbered 404 the horse was like a bright chesnut in colour and stood 15.3 hands. Today the breed is of the same colour with a little white allowed on the face. The head is big with a broad forehead and joined by a graceful neck to a deep round body which is wide in front and behind. The legs are straight with big knees and large feet. The walk must be 'smart and fine' and the trot 'well balanced all round'; the average height is 16 hands.

The Suffolk is noted for both early maturity and

Suffolk Punch

longevity. One stallion was recorded as travelling for twenty-five years without a break, and a mare produced a foal every year for sixteen consecutive years. The horses did all the work on most East Anglian farms. In Suffolk in 1939 there were no less than 18,238 horses, nearly all Suffolks, at work on the farms. In towns also these horses have always been much in demand for drawing brewers' drays, and the Army once used them for dragging artillery into action.

Suffolk stallions are extensively used for crossing with smaller mares and many chesnut hunters owe their colour and stamina to Suffolk blood.

The hereditary weakness of weak side-bones in the hoof has now been eradicated by careful breeding.

Exmoor Pony Exmoor is a high, wild, windy plateau in the western part of Somerset and the sandstone uplands form one of the ten National Parks in Britain. It is also the home of this exceptional breed which emanated from Alaska and finally reached the South of England via Iberia, Europe, and across the land-bridge that then joined the British Isles to the mainland.

As can be expected from such an ancestry this Celtic breed is well adapted to harsh conditions. The winter coat has two layers and a fan of tail hair which hangs over the first two or three joints of the tail and prevents

Exmoor Pony

the rain running down the animal's hindquarters. Likewise the eyes are protected from lashing rain by special lids. The nostrils are large and, when expanded, allow the pony to inhale ample air to sustain a long gallop.

The ponies are thickset, deep-chested with sturdy hind legs. The colours are bay, brown, or dun with mealy markings on the muzzle and round the eyes. There are no white points. Mares do not exceed 12·2 hands and stallions 12·3.

All ponies in this country are branded on the shoulder with the herd number and their own number on the hindquarters. The breeding and the gathering in October of the ponies are in the hands of the Commoners who have rights of grazing on the moor. Surplus stock is sold at the annual Bampton Fair.

The Exmoor ponies were used as pack-ponies, in traps, and for riding. Many must be the Exmoor child who has been taken to school on a pony. Today the breed is seen in driving classes at shows, and ridden by children competing in all manner of events. It is also well suited for pony-trekking and endurance riding. The Colonel, winner of the Grand National Steeplechase in 1863, was a part Exmoor stallion.

SHEEP

Boreray Scotland has a notable collection of historic breeds of sheep whose preservation is due to their remote island homes. Of the three breeds found in the Western Isles two, the Soay and Boreray, still flourish on islands within the St Kilda group.

In 1930 the St Kildans were evacuated from their island at their own request but their flocks of sheep on

Boreray Sheep

neighbouring Boreray were not removed and their descendants are still there. Access to the island is hazardous and the flock survives without the presence of man. The sheep are, therefore, feral and only in 1971 were three ewes and three rams taken off the island and made available for research at Roslin near Edinburgh. It is likely that the Boreray represents a cross between Black-faces and the Old Scottish Shortwool and is similar to present-day commercial breeds in appearance and fleece qualities. Two-thirds of the population of about 680 have off-white fleeces, one fifth grey, and the balance tan or blackish. Often there is a dark collar that extends from the nape of the neck to the forelegs. All the sheep are horned, the tups sporting huge, spiralling horns up to seventy-five centimetres in length.

They have the behavioural sense to avoid the worst of the weather and make full use of 'cleits', stone beehive shelters built by the islanders to dry the carcasses of seabirds.

Castlemilk Moorit It was not until November 1983 that this breed was classified as 'critically rare' with less than eighty breeding females in existence. As late as 1970 the whole breed could have been lost if two far-sighted sheep-breeders had not been at a dispersal sale in Scotland when the last remaining flock was put 'under the hammer' and destined for the slaughterhouse. The Rare Breeds Survival Trust did not then exist.

Castlemilk Moorit Sheep

These sheep were bred by a Scottish landowner, Sir Jock Buchanan-Jardine, on his Castlemilk estate near Lockerbie in Dumfries, and described as 'Moorit Shetlands', a name which is now altered to avoid confusion with the true Shetland sheep of that reddish colour.

These Moorit Shetlands and pale-coloured Soays were used to create the breed with, at some stage, an introduction of Manx Loghtan blood. Because of the very stout horns carried by the rams there must also be some Moufflon blood in them as well. The breed now resembles a giant, blond Soay. There is little colour variation and the wool is close and soft, ideal for hand-spinning.

Cotswold For this large, polled breed we have to thank the Romans who brought with them their long-woolled sheep in the first century AD. What is now known as the Cotswold Lion breed adapted well to the limestone hills east of the Severn Estuary and became the mainstay of the woollen trade for which the Cotswolds were famous. The name itself derives from 'wold', the Old English for a bare hill, and 'cote', the wattle enclosure used by the shepherds for penning their sheep.

The Woolsack upon which the Lord Chancellor sits in Parliament is even now stuffed with Cotswold wool! Crossing with the Leicester breed, itself descended from the Roman imports, improved the Cotswold in the eighteenth century. New breeds were created through other crosses. The Oxford Down is the result of a cross between the Cotswold and Hampshire Down, and the Oldenberg likewise is a German Marsh sheep crossed with a Cotswold.

Cotswold Sheep

The import of cheaper wool from Australia and the rejection of mutton by the English market caused the steady decline of this breed and only the dedication of one particular breeder, and now an active breed society, has saved the historic Cotswold from extinction.

The sheep are easily identified by the prominent tuft or forelock of wool that is always left unclipped. The rams continue to be in demand for crossing with other breeds.

Hebridean This breed, once erroneously called St Kilda, now no longer inhabits the Hebrides, its original home. The earliest report of these sheep 'with the biggest horns' was in 1703 when they were found on islands north of North Uist. Then the sheep had four to six horns apiece and were coloured black through russet to white; some were even multi-coloured.

Today the breed, either black or dark brown, is usually found in parks on the mainland as an ornamental feature. It belongs to the Northern Short-Tailed group of sheep like the Soay – that lives on St Kilda – and the Shetland, and is classed as 'primitive'. A small sheep with long legs, fine bones, and multi-horned, it is very hardy and able to thrive on poor pastures. The fleece is long and much in demand by hand-spinners. When crossed with long-woolled or Down breeds, such as the Suffolk, excellent lambs are the result.

Like most primitive breeds the meat is both sweet and lean. Because of its increasing popularity the Hebridean will soon follow its near-relative, the Jacob, and be taken off the list of threatened breeds.

Leicester Longwool From its native Midlands pastures this breed had, by the eighteenth century, spread to most parts of the country and was used by Robert Bakewell of Derby, the master breeder of that time, as the stock for his famous experiments in cross-breeding. Bakewell made his fortune hiring out pure-bred rams to other breeders requiring new blood in their flocks. Such is the change in fashion the Leicester is now a rare breed, and confined to the Yorkshire wolds. It is a large, polled, white-faced sheep with a heavy fleece of curly, lustrous wool. A hardy breed, its greatest asset is the ability to produce first-class rams for crossing.

Leicester Longwool Sheep

New breeds created by the Leicester are the Wensleydale (× Teeswater or Durham), Lleyn (× Welsh Mountain), Border Leicester (× Cheviot), and the Ile de France (× Rambouillet).

Flocks of Leicesters are found in Australia and New Zealand, and a breed flock-book is kept in Australia.

Lincoln Longwool Until the end of the eighteenth century when Merino wool began to appear in the British markets, sent from Spain and Australia, the Lincoln Longwool sheep accounted for about half the

Lincoln Longwool Sheep

long-wool clip. The wool was the longest and the most lustrous in the country with a staple length of between ten and eighteen inches. One fleece turned the scales at twenty-nine pounds in 1730 and even today the Lincolnshire word 'far-welted' is used to describe a sheep carrying a massive fleece.

The Lincoln is the largest breed and well adapted to grazing on marshy land in cold, windy conditions. It is also very much a dual-purpose breed; the wool in demand for lustre yarns and the skins for rugs. The rams are used for siring heavyweight lambs. The breed is able to survive as a good carcass is provided for the butcher and the fleece can also command a fair price.

The sheep carry no horns and have white faces with a heavy forelock falling over the eyes.

The breed has been exported for many years – more than 45,000 since the start of this century. In 1906 a ram was sold to an Argentine breeder for no less than 1,450 guineas. The Russians are also keen buyers.

Manx Loghtan This breed closely resembles the Hebridean and was undoubtedly introduced to the Isle of Man by the Vikings who used that island as a springboard from which to penetrate the north-west

Manx Loghtan Sheep

regions of the British Isles. The word 'loghtan' is Manx for a light-brown (mouse) colour and correctly describes the fleece colour of this breed which is short-woolled and short-tailed. The legs are bare of wool.

Fragments of a woollen cloak from a Viking grave on the Isle of Man were almost certainly made from a fleece of a direct ancestor of the present Manx sheep.

The breed is renowned for growing two, four or even six horns each and the rams are always horned. All writers about the breed remark on the sweetness and excellence of the mutton.

In 1984 the Interbreed Sheep Champion at the Rare Breeds Show was a two-year-old Manx Loghtan ewe, a great achievement for a 'primitive' breed.

North Ronaldsay The seaweed diet of these sheep living on the island of North Ronaldsay, the most

North Ronaldsay Sheep

northerly of the Orkney Island, is their most striking feature. Closely related to the Shetland, they spend much of their time on the beaches and among the rocks looking for kelp and the edible 'dulse' which are the most nutritious species of seaweed. The ewes are only allowed inside the wooden wall that protects the precious grassland during lambing time.

The flock is a unique remnant of the large flocks of Orkney sheep that were kept on common lands. They are descended from the short-tailed sheep of Scandinavia with a pronounced 'dish' face. The rams have large, curled horns; the ewes are polled.

In 1973 the Rare Breeds Survival Trust acquired Linga Holm, a small island west of Stronsay, and a small reserve flock of North Ronaldsay was established on it.

Nine colours of wool can be identified within a flock including that of 'skimlet' (greyish brown).

Portland This breed has the doubtful distinction of being the rarest in the country because of its low prolificacy. Seldom are twins born and the lambing percentages are low. It can, however, lamb at various times in the year.

It is a small sheep, closely related to the Welsh Mountain and a descendant of the native tan-faced British breeds. The lambs are reddish brown at birth but the fleece soon changes to white. The legs are brown or tan, and the nose pink, an unusual characteristic. Both sexes are horned, the horns of the rams show Merino influence by being spiralled.

The meat is of exceptional flavour.

The breed takes its name from the rocky Isle of Portland off the Dorset coast and shares with the

Portland Sheep

Herdwick of the Cumbrian fells the fictitious honour of having been brought over on ships of the Spanish Armada. The sheep were said to have swum ashore when the galleons were wrecked.

Shetland These small sheep are relics of the Iron Age, which began about 500 BC, and are similar to Scandinavian sheep which were introduced by the Norse settlers in the ninth century AD. The traditional identification system of earmarks, still used today in Norway and Iceland, goes back over a thousand years. Until the nineteenth century the ewes were regularly milked. Where there is access to the seashore the sheep will often eat seaweed when grass is unobtainable.

White is now the predominant wool colour but other natural shades are 'moorit' (reddish), black, 'sheila' (grey), and brown. The fleeces were traditionally harvested in June and the wool plucked rather than shorn – this was called 'rooing'.

Today the quality of Shetland wool is the basis of the renowned cottage industry of the islands. The hand-made lace shawls from Uist that can be drawn through a wedding ring, and the Fair Isle patterned sweaters are world-famous.

Ewes are usually polled and noted for their longevity – even at fifteen years of age they can produce twin lambs. The rams carry light horns.

A breed society was formed in 1926 to preserve pure-bred stock.

Shetland Sheep

Shropshire As the name implies this handsome member of the Down group of sheep evolved from the fine-woolled, horned Morfe Common sheep, and a black-faced, horned breed found on the Long Mynd and Cannock Chase. The introduction of Southdown and Leicester blood improved the cross which was recognised as a separate breed for the first time in 1882.

At the beginning of this century the Shropshire was exported in great numbers, especially to the United

Shropshire Sheep

States, but this market collapsed in 1930 due to a serious foot-and-mouth epidemic in this country. The breeders were unable to interest the English flock-masters in this small sheep with a heavily woolled head and breed numbers dropped drastically.

The hardiest and most prolific of the Down breeds, the Shropshire has a black face with a generous covering of wool on the poll. The eye spectacles, ears, and legs are also black. The fleece of short wool is dense.

The breed continues to enjoy great popularity abroad and its future, therefore, is not really in doubt.

Soay These primitive sheep are probably similar to the earliest types of domesticated sheep in northern Europe and bear a close resemblance to the wild Moufflon (*Ovis musimon*) of Corsica and Sardinia.

The name Soay is Old Norse for 'sheep island' and only on this island in the Outer Hebrides and neighbouring Hirta do the sheep exist in their feral state. Small breeding groups have been exported to the Continent and North America to serve as vital reservoirs of unique genetic material.

The rams develop a dark, hairy mane and have heavy, curved horns. The ewes can either be polled or horned. The predominant colour is dark brown but the belly and chest are lighter coloured. Like other primitive breeds the fleece has an abundance of hair which gives the animal a rough appearance.

The Soays are great wanderers and hard to 'turn' by fencing. They are partial to a diet of seaweed on their native shores, choosing only those species that contain the most protein. They are naturally very hardy, agile, and great jumpers.

Soay Sheep

Wensleydale The breed is said to have originated in 1838 from a cross between ewes of an old type found in the Wensleydale area of Yorkshire and a Dishley Leicester ram. Among the progeny was the ram Blue Cap, the first recorded animal with the blue face and ears now so typical of this breed.

It is a large, long-woolled sheep with a lustrous, curly fleece and ringlets over the face. Hardy, with no horns, it fattens well on arable land and roots.

The main function of the breed has always been to produce rams for crossing on draft Swaledale ewes, the resultant cross being called a 'Masham'. More recently the Teeswater rams have been preferred for this cross-breeding and the numbers of pure Wensleydales have dropped alarmingly.

Wensleydale Sheep

The white, lustrous fleece, devoid of any kemp, and blue skin pigmentation make the breed very suitable for tropical countries where heat stress and sunburn cause problems. The breed is, therefore, found in the West Indies and has been used to improve stock in many other countries.

White-Faced Woodland One of the largest of the hill breeds, long-legged and horned with a white face and pink nostrils. The breed can trace its ancestry back to the black-faced, horned group of sheep that could have been introduced by the Vikings who settled along the east coast of northern Britain. These sheep were

White-Faced Woodland Sheep

confined to the eastern Pennines and concentrated around the Derbyshire market town of Pennistone. The tenants of the Duke of Devonshire, the local large landowner, owned many of the sheep and the Duke saw to it that the breed was improved by crossing with Merino rams imported by George III – 'Farmer George'.

The breed is dual-purpose, able to produce heavy lambs as well as carry a fine fleece well suited for felt used for hats. Their tails are particularly strong. The rams are in demand for crossing with their related black-faced, horned, hill breeds, such as the Swaledale, to produce a speckle-faced ewe.

The breed is now found far beyond Woodland Dale and is not in danger.

Wiltshire Horn The ancestry of this breed can be traced back to the white-faced, horned group of breeds of south-west England, which includes the Dorset Horn and the Exmoor Horn. One of their characteristics is that both ewes and rams carry horns. In 1724 Defoe

Wiltshire Horn Sheep

recorded flocks of up to 5,000 on the Wiltshire downlands; the dung of this hardy sheep on land to be ploughed was the most valued product in the days before farming practice changed from arable to pastoral.

By the mid 1700s there was a need for a more efficient meat-producer and the Southdown breed was preferred, at first only for crossing and then in its pure-bred form. Numbers of the Wiltshire Horn fell drastically.

The Wiltshire Horn grows little or no wool and the fleece, mainly a thick mat of hair on the back, peels off as the sheep fatten. This occurs in no other breed, and, together with the white skin pigmentation, makes the sheep well suited to warmer climates. There are no problems with maggots in the fleece. A healthy export trade has, therefore, developed in this breed which are now found in Zimbabwe, crossed with Persian sheep, and in Malaysia. They are also very popular in Australia.

In Britain the Wiltshire Horn Sheep Society was formed in 1923 and the breed can be considered safe. The rams are used for crossing with Welsh ewes and the crosses demonstrate the breed's ability to produce prime early lambs or mutton off grass without the need to feed concentrates.

GOATS

Bagot A semi-feral herd which lived in Bagots Park, Staffordshire, accounted for most of the breed for many years until these animals were donated to the Rare Breeds Survival Trust. To help build up this rarest breed of goats small herds have been established in various parts of the country, including Wimpole Hall

Opposite: *Bagot Goat*

near Cambridge. Descendants of the Staffordshire herd are also found in the park at Levens Hall in Cumbria, an historic house owned by the Bagot family on whose coat of arms the goat has appeared since the fourteenth century.

One theory is that the Bagot goats originated from animals brought to Britain by the Crusaders from the Rhône Valley in Switzerland where a similar breed, the Schwartzhal, is still to be found.

The preferred colouring is black head, neck, and shoulders with the rest of the body white. This is rarely achieved in practice and most Bagots have dark markings on the hindquarters and a white blaze, while the black usually does not extend over the entire forequarters. The hair is long and both sexes are horned.

Bagots can neither be classed as dairy animals nor as producers of good meat or pelts. Their worth lies in their long historical associations and their attractive appearance.

Golden Guernsey It is not the 'golden goat' of Syria as recorded by Herodotus but a 'made' breed based on a local, common goat origin and the result of an infusion of Anglo-Nubian and British Alpine blood.

A medium-sized goat with silky, short or long golden hair on the body, face, and legs. The skin is also golden. The ears, which are large, have a distinctive upward and outward turn at their tips. The breed is horned but most animals have the horn buds removed early in life. In Guernsey the horns are usually left to grow as a means of defence.

The breed is robust and hardy but its milk yield does not compare with other popular breeds.

Golden Guernsey Goat

CATTLE

Belted Galloway The most distinctive feature of this hardy beef breed from south-west Scotland is the broad white band which encircles the middle part of the body. This 'belt' is thought to have been inherited from a Dutch breed, the Lakevelder, imported during the sixteenth century. The 'belted' Sheeted Somerset is now extinct but both this breed and the Belted Welsh Black survive.

Before the advent of the railways the beef cattle from Galloway and Dumfries were driven to the markets in Norfolk and the drovers always liked to have a 'beltie' among the herd as the white stood out well in the gloom or darkness.

Since 1945 the breed has been much in demand overseas and in the United States there is an association for the breeders of 'belties'. The cattle are also well established in Argentina and Brazil.

The Belted Galloway is a good crossing breed in both sexes, the progeny always being polled. In colder climes the cattle grow a thick, shaggy coat of hair.

British White It is not known whether the earliest white cattle in Britain were indigenous or imported from Italy by the Romans. Some relationship exists between this breed and the herds of wild white cattle which

Below: *British White Cow*

Opposite: *Belted Galloway Cow*

survive at Chillingham and elsewhere, although the feral cattle are horned unlike the polled British White. The British White is, however, very similar to the Swedish mountain breed – the Fjallras – and there is a strong presumption that the breed could have been introduced by the Vikings.

The breed, once widely distributed and especially strong in East Anglia, was becoming rare when its breed society was formed soon after the First World War.

It is a dual-purpose breed, closely resembling the Dairy Shorthorn. The colour is white with black ears, nose, eyelashes, and feet with sometimes black flecks on other parts of the hide. This colour combination renders the breed tolerant to heat and it is interesting to note that the nomadic Fulani of the Sahel and northern Nigeria keep cattle that have the same coloration.

The British White has been exported to Colombia, Kenya, Canada, Uruguay and most recently to Australia and North America where its tolerance to heat is a highly prized asset.

Chillingham The Chillingham cattle are unique in their antiquity and the wild state in which they continue to live. Chillingham Park lies in Glendale in Northumberland, fifty miles north of Newcastle. The park was probably enclosed about 1225 and the vegetation remaining within it has changed little since medieval times; only the size of the park has been seriously diminished.

The first record of these wild cattle dates from 1689

Chillingham Cattle

but they must have been roaming in the lawless Border country before then. Certainly wild cattle were hunted by the monarchs within the Chillingham and other parks such as Cadzow and Chartley until the seventeenth century. The herd at Chillingham has remained completely pure and the natural laws of selection prevail. These cattle are, therefore, smaller, more primitive, and with greater resistance to disease than the other white breeds. Their colour is white with reddish-brown ears, nose, and feet.

The average life of the cow is twelve years, and that of the bull ten years.

The herd numbers have remained fairly constant this century – forty-five in 1930 and fifty-five in 1979. Today there are sixty cattle. In 1947 the harsh winter was too much even for the hardy Chillingham breed and, despite some feeding, nineteen animals died.

A reserve herd has now been established in the north of Scotland.

Dexter The smallest of the British breeds weighing when mature between six and eight hundredweight and standing about thirty-nine inches to the back of the neck. They can be either long- or short-legged, and carry horns on a short, broad head. Colour is usually black but they can also be either red or dun.

The origins of the breed are uncertain but they were the traditional Irish house cow and could have derived from a cross between Kerry and Devon cattle. They were first seen in England in 1882. This is a true miniature breed, but is not of great genetical purity.

A hardy breed, their winter coats grow quickly and the hair covers the udders for added protection. They calve easily and show good resistance to diseases such as brucellosis and mastitis. Above all they are economical feeders and, therefore, ideally suited to smallholdings, able to produce efficiently both milk and meat.

Dexter Cattle

Gloucester This breed was one of the most prominent dairy breeds from the eleventh to the nineteenth centuries. Gloucestershire has long been famous for its cheeses – Double Gloucester and Blue Vinney, for

Opposite: *Gloucester Cattle*

example – all of which were made from the milk of the Gloucester cattle. In 1796 Edward Jenner made the first anti-smallpox serum from the blood of a Gloucester cow whose skin has been carefully preserved.

The advent of the Longhorns and the Shorthorns nearly caused the demise of the breed which, by 1970, numbered a mere fifty cows.

Helped by a new breed society and the formation of several small herds the breed is now well on the way to recovery.

An attractive animal, the Gloucester is dark brown in colour with a white stripe along the back and hindquarters, and down the tail. The bulls are darker and carry a distinctive crest. The horns on both sexes are forward facing and of medium length.

Below: *Irish Moiled Cow*

Irish Moiled The most endangered cattle breed in the British Isles, the Irish Moiled is one of the two native breeds of Ireland – the other being the Kerry – and reputed to be descended from stock brought over by the Vikings. In 1983 only thirty-one animals of full pedigree remained.

A meeting of farmers in 1926 in Belfast established the breed society for the purpose of 'retaining the best of what remained of our native Ulster cattles as a patriotic duty'.

The cow is distinguished by a white stripe, known as 'finching', that runs the full length of the back; a white tail, white underline and udder. The flanks and neck are roan or red.

The cattle are polled.

Kerry The breed neared extinction in 1981 when the State-owned herd at Muckross in Eire was reduced to a mere fifty cattle, a number too small for the selection of bulls from milk-recorded dams, and the full tally of registered cows and heifers in that year was 189. Probably the same number may have survived unregistered.

The breed takes its name from the south-west county of Eire, Kerry, and has been traditionally kept in that county as the house cow. It is a dual-purpose animal, able to thrive on marginal land and survive under sparse feeding conditions in cold, wet places. These cattle live long and respond well to favourable environments.

The cow is small and black, but in the past the influence of imported Longhorns, and then Shorthorns from England, produced colour variations, including the white 'finch' or stripe along the back. Occasionally

Kerry Cow

white is found on the udder. The breed is horned, the horns being white with black tips. Their appearance is akin to that of the native cattle of south-west France and Spain to which they are distantly related.

Longhorn The origin of this ancient breed is uncertain; it may be related to the Criollo cattle of Spain or be an indigenous descendant of the wild aurochs of northern Europe. It has been known in Ireland for centuries but may have been imported from the western parts of Britain where it was most commonly found.

When first improved by breeders in West Yorkshire it was known as the 'Craven Longhorn'. In the eighteenth century Robert Bakewell transformed the Longhorn from a good triple-purpose animal into a specialist beef

strain. By 1800 the breed was probably the most popular in the British Isles, but this popularity was short-lived and it had to give way before the relentless advance of the smaller Hereford and Angus breeds. Today the value of the Longhorn as a beef sire is now recognised and the quality of the beef is excellent. Milk yields are not heavy but the milk is very rich with a high butterfat content.

It is a massive, powerful animal with a long body and rather short legs. The long and usually down-curved horns give the breed a deceptively menacing appearance. The colour is brindle with perhaps a bluish tinge; the tail and stripe along the back are white, and white also appears on the legs, dewlap, and the flanks.

Red Poll When the herd-book for this excellent dual-purpose breed was first published in 1873 the name used was the Norfolk and Suffolk Red Polled. The breed was the result of a cross between the Suffolk Dun and similar red cattle from neighbouring Norfolk. The cattle are of a deep red colour with a white tail-switch and some white on the udder. The head is broad and hornless; the body long and deep and carried on short legs.

The Red Poll has a reputation for thrift and hardiness as well as longevity. Records show that four times as many Red Polls lived to have a tenth calf as the average of all other breeds. In 1955 the breed produced the Champion Cow at the London Dairy Show, while at Smithfield Red Polls had the largest entry of any breed. Truly a general farmer's cow!

The cows calve easily and have a great will to live, unlike the Friesians which to a large extent have been responsible for the rapid decline of the Red Poll. Should

Opposite: *Longhorn Bull*

Red Poll Bull

the fashion for keeping pure dairy and beef herds change, there is every chance that the Red Poll will once again become popular. In fact, the breed has recently expanded in number and has been removed from the list of rare breeds in danger.

Shetland Their origin, most probably Scandinavian, is not definitely known but these cattle have existed on the Shetland Islands as a distinct breed, akin to the Jersey, for several hundred years.

Once their colouring ranged from black and white to red and white, dun, and mottle grey. Today the predominant and preferred colour is black and white which has given rise to the false conclusion that Friesian

Shetland Bull

blood had infiltrated pure-breed Shetland stock. When not carrying their thick winter coats these cattle can easily be mistaken for Friesians but are smaller, shorter, and more compact. The horns are slender and curved, the skin soft, and the meat full of flavour.

The value of the breed to produce first crosses is well recognised. They are good dual-purpose cattle and make excellent single sucklers in harsh conditions. They calve easily but do suffer from poor fertility due to inbreeding, which is why their numbers remain low.

White Park About 700 years ago much of Britain was covered by forest and wild cattle were prized beasts of the chase. When Henry III of England granted a Charter to certain of his nobles to enclose extensive tracts of forest as hunting parks it was natural that the wild cattle should also be enclosed along with the deer and boar. The feral herd at Chillingham in Northumberland still roams its original park. Other domesticated herds are found at Dynevor in Wales and Cadzow in Scotland.

The White Park is a distinctive and attractive animal, white in colour with black ears, nose, eyelids, feet, and teats. The head is of medium length and broad, with long horns which sweep out and upwards. The skin is fine and may be slightly pigmented as befits a breed which originated in a hotter climate.

In the Second World War, in order to safeguard the future of the breed, a group of representative cattle was sent to the United States and a small herd still flourishes on the King Ranch in Texas.

The breed is notable for its colour-marking ability and possesses valuable commercial characteristics. It is

Opposite: *White Park Bull*

a beef breed and the cross-bred progeny show considerable hybrid vigour thus making the White Park a valuable beef sire.

The cows have strongly developed maternal instincts and are able to thrive on low-quality feed.

PIGS

Berkshire A traditional pork pig – short-bodied, short-legged and with a dished face characteristic of Chinese and Neapolitan pigs introduced to Britain in the late eighteenth century. The original 'Berkshire' was coloured red and black but the predominant colour is now black and often with white on the legs and face. The ears are now pricked and not lop as was the earlier breed.

Berkshires have always been popular in the United

Berkshire Pig

States – in 1980 a boar was sold for the equivalent of £4,000 – Japan, and Australia, and semen from overseas stock can, therefore, be used for strengthening the small numbers that remain in the United Kingdom. It is an ideal pig for the cottager and repays good housing and feeding. Like the Tamworth it is regarded as a 'bright' pig and keeps its owners on their toes!

Berkshires suffer from the stigma of other black breeds of having blue tainted meat but when crossed with a Large White they produce a white carcass. The breed society was formed in 1885.

British Lop Once known as the Long White Lop-eared it is closely related to the pigs of Scandinavia and the Welsh breed, collectively described as 'Landrace' and essentially bacon pigs.

Traditionally the British Lop was a small West

British Lop Pig

Country pig that was kept in order to eat the rubbish. It was ideal for the beginner or a person only wanting to keep one or two pigs.

Excellent sows, they produce large litters without the aids of rails or lights. One sow was recorded as producing seventeen pigs from its twenty-first litter; and the average number of piglets reared from 3,000 recorded litters of this breed was 9·2. They can live outside throughout the year and thrive on a predominantly cereal diet.

The appearance of the 'Landrace' is white, long-bodied, and long-eared. The British Lop carries very prominent lop-ears and was once one of the largest British breeds in size.

Gloucester Old Spot Pig

Gloucester Old Spot A dual-purpose, mainly bacon pig which can be killed at any weight. It is also hardy and thrifty having evolved in the specialised environment of the Vale of Berkeley in Gloucestershire where its purpose was to convert by-products of whey and windfall apples into meat.

The Old Spot is a great rooter and scavenger; ringing is, therefore, essential. It grows a thick winter coat and can live out all year. The sows are prolific, farrow easily, and once held the national record for the number of litters per sow – twenty-four – and the highest number of piglets reared per litter.

It is a large lop-eared pig with a white coat sparsely sprinkled with black spots, and is used extensively for crossing with Large White and Landrace pigs to produce a leaner carcass.

Large Black Until the beginning of this century sows of this breed were found in nearly every farm in the country and especially in the West Country where the apples, and in East Anglia the surplus cereals, proved plentiful.

The preference for lean, white breeds kept intensively inside caused the great decline of the breed with its distinctive jowl, large hams, and forward-carried lop-ears. However the innate qualities of docility, hardiness, and low-cost food conversion are now beginning to be appreciated once again and the Large Black will come into its own when pigs are required to live and grow well outside on low-protein rations.

The sow can be mated with boars of white breeds and the resultant hybrid pig has the favoured blue and white coloration, and grows well.

Large Black Pig

Middle White The breed, first recognised officially in 1882, evolved from a cross between a Large White and the Small, or China White pigs. It is believed that the fat China pig, from which the Middle White derives its distinctive and genetically dominant dished head, came to this country in the holds of the sailing-ships on the Far Eastern run. They were kept on board to provide fresh meat.

The stronghold of the breed was Yorkshire. It was always a poor man's pig, being quiet, easy to keep, and producing a fine, fat carcass. Traditionally two pigs were kept at the bottom of the garden, one to fatten and probably kill before the winter, and the other to sell. It is the nearest in the minority breeds to an intensive pig, disliking mud and preferring to be inside. The shape is short, wide, and compact with heavy jowls and pricked ears.

Middle Whites once comprised over half the pig

Middle White Pig

Middle White Pig

population of Japan, and pedigree stock from this country has helped found herds in South America, Africa, Malaya, and Austria.

Tamworth One of the most distinctive pig breeds in appearance, the Tamworth is of an attractive red-gold colour with a long snout and prick ears.

Controversy surrounds the origin of the colour and the most likely explanation is that Sir Robert Peel, the Member of Parliament for Stafford in 1812, imported a red Barbadian boar and crossed it with the local grey semi-wild pigs. Alternatively Sir Robert's neighbour,

Sir Francis Lawley of Tamworth, received as a present from India a wild, red boar.

Whatever its origin the 'Tamworth' breed was well established by 1885 when the first herd-book was formed. Herds were set up in the United States, Canada, and Australia. The pigs were kept in a semi-wild state, rooting for acorns and beechmast, and this may account for their small litters. They thrive outdoors and are valuable for reclaiming scrub and rough pasture.

The breed matures late, is harder to manage than other breeds, and objects to ringing which prevents digging. A Tamworth is regarded as a 'bright' pig, needing strict control and disliking intensely solitary confinement. The piglets are born with black stripes on the flanks; this is a characteristic of the litters of wild boar.

Tamworth Pig

POULTRY

All breeds of poultry probably had as their ancestor the wild Red Jungle Fowl which is found in the jungles of India and South-east Asia. The resultant cross-breeds were all adapted over the centuries for a specific purpose – notably for meat production, cock-fighting or, more recently, for egg production.

The domestic fowl was known in China 3,400 years ago and from there spread westwards through Mesopotamia and Greece to Europe. The Romans brought their poultry with them to Britain and, much later, fowl were introduced to North America by the Spanish invaders and the Pilgrim Fathers. The South American continent had fowl imported directly from Asia and the resultant Aracauna breed is today distinguished by the green and blue eggs they lay. There are a few ancient breeds still found in Britain. Probably the most famous is the Dorking whose ancestry can be traced back to Roman times, but most of the breeds associated with the 'old farmyard' were actually created after 1850. The well-known Orpington is one of these, and a Black Orpington holds the world individual egg-laying record – a hen in New Zealand laid 361 eggs in 364 days.

It was in 1847 that the first Cochin fowls which resembled the present standard for that breed were imported from Shanghai; they came on the poultry scene like giants. Today they are found in six different colours and in the United States in three more besides.

Poultry breeds come and go quickly, slaves to the dictates of fashion and the commercial world. The popular mid-twentieth-century breeds such as the Rhode Island Red, the White Leghorn, and the Sussex

Opposite: *Welsummer Cock*